W9-BYG-308

47

AMERICAN HOLIDAYS

Cinco de Mayo

Leia Tait

Weigl Publishers Inc.

Published by Weigl Publishers Inc.
350 5th Avenue, Suite 3304, PMB 6G
New York, NY 10118-0069
Web site: www.weigl.com

Copyright ©2007 WEIGL PUBLISHERS INC.
All rights reserved. No part of this publication may be reproduced,
stored in a retrieval system, or transmitted in any form or by any means,
electronic, mechanical, photocopying, recording, or otherwise, without
the prior written permission of the publisher.

Library of Congress Cataloging-in-Publication Data

Tait, Leia.
    Cinco de mayo / Leia Tait.
        p. cm. -- (American holidays)
    Includes index.
    ISBN 1-59036-460-0 (hard cover : alk. paper) -- ISBN
1-59036-463-5 (soft cover : alk. paper)
    1. Cinco de Mayo (Mexican holiday)--Juvenile literature.
2. Mexico--Social life and customs--Juvenile literature. 3. Mexican
Americans--Social life and customs--Juvenile literature. 4. Cinco
de Mayo, Battle of, Puebla, Mexico, 1862--Juvenile literature.
    I. Title.
F1233.T175 2006
394.262--dc22   2005029035

Printed in the United States of America
1 2 3 4 5 6 7 8 9 0 10 09 08 07 06

Editor Heather C. Hudak
Design and Layout Terry Paulhus

Cover During Cinco de Mayo,
dancers perform at celebrations
in Los Angeles, California.

All of the Internet URLs given in the book were valid at the time of
publication. However, due to the dynamic nature of the Internet, some
addresses may have changed, or sites may have ceased
to exist since publication. While the author and publisher regret any
inconvenience this may cause readers, no responsibility for any such
changes can be accepted by either the author or
the publisher.

Every reasonable effort has been made to trace ownership and to obtain
permission to reprint copyright material. The publishers would be
pleased to have any errors or omissions brought to their attention so
that they may be corrected in subsequent printings.

Contents

Introduction

★ ★

Cinco de Mayo celebrates the Mexican victory at the Battle of Puebla.

Every year on May 5, Cinco de Mayo is celebrated across Mexico and the United States. Crowds gather in city streets to hear lively music. They join in parades and watch colorful dance shows. They eat tasty foods made just for the event. Children dress in festive costumes and perform traditional songs and dances. People decorate their homes and public buildings with bright flowers and Mexican flags. On Cinco de Mayo, people find many exciting ways to celebrate being Mexican.

Cinco de Mayo is Spanish for "the fifth of May." This holiday celebrates the victory of the Mexican army over the French at *La Batalla de Puebla,* or the Battle of Puebla. Mexicans and Mexican Americans began celebrating this holiday more than 100 years ago. Today, it is a symbol of their courage, strength, and unity.

DID YOU KNOW?

People have lived in Mexico and Central America for almost 23,000 years. Cultures that are native to these areas are called Mesoamerican.

The Aztec peoples founded the Mexican empire. Ancient Aztec traditions are an important part of Cinco de Mayo celebrations.

Mexico in Danger

★ ★

The emperor of France wanted to control Mexico.

I n 1861, Mexico owed money to many countries. President Benito Juárez needed time to pay it back. He asked the rulers of Britain, Spain, and France for two years to repay Mexico's debts. The rulers of Great Britain and Spain agreed. The emperor of France, Napoleon III, did not want to wait. He decided that he wanted more than just the money. He wanted to take control of all of Mexico.

Napoleon III sent his army to conquer Mexico. It was one of the strongest armies in the world. It had not lost a battle in more than 50 years. The French troops were well trained, and they had the newest equipment. General Conde de Lorencez led the French army. Napoleon III was sure France would win.

DID YOU KNOW?

The French army invaded Veracruz, Mexico, in 1861. It began marching to Mexico City. The Mexican people met the army at Puebla.

Mexico on the Map

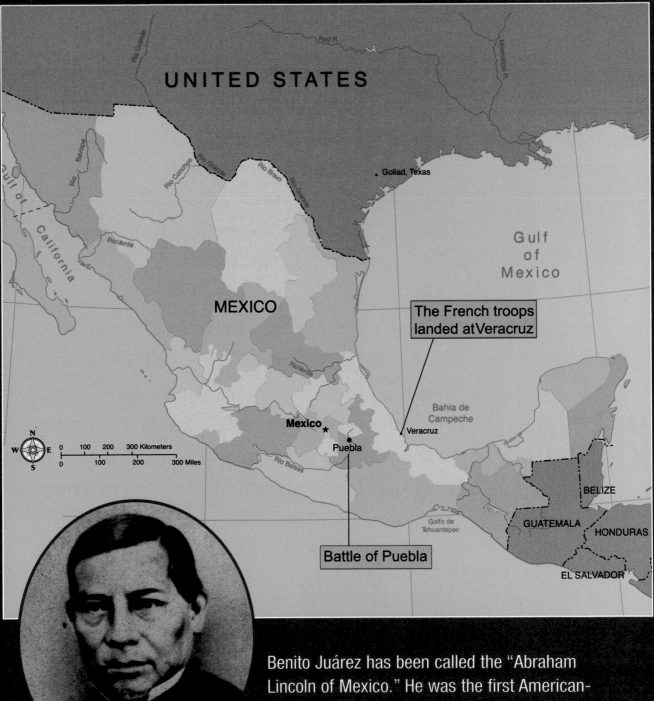

UNITED STATES

Rio Grande

Red R.

Mississippi R.

Gulf of California

Rio Bavispe

Rio

Rio Conchos

Rio Grande

Rio Bravo

Rio Grande

Goliad, Texas

RioVerde

MEXICO

Gulf of Mexico

RioVerde

The French troops landed at Veracruz

Bahia de Campeche

Veracruz

Mexico ★

Puebla

Rio Balsas

N W E S

| 0 | 100 | 200 | 300 Kilometers |
| 0 | 100 | 200 | 300 Miles |

Golfo de Tehuantepec

BELIZE

GUATEMALA

HONDURAS

Battle of Puebla

EL SALVADOR

Benito Juárez has been called the "Abraham Lincoln of Mexico." He was the first American-Indian president of Mexico. Mexico is located south of the United States.

Battle of Puebla

Many Mexican fighters carried farm tools for weapons.

The Mexican people learned of Napoleon's attack. They formed an army to fight the French. Most of the troops were farmers with no military training. They carried knives and farm tools for weapons. Local *Zapotec* and *Mestizo* Indians also came to join the battle. Even with their help, the French had many more troops than the Mexicans.

The two armies met near the city of Puebla on May 5, 1862. The Mexican army was led by Ignacio Zaragoza. The Mexicans attacked the French army with their **cavalry**. Then they released a stampede of cattle to trample the French soldiers. After four hours of fighting, the French army was forced to retreat. The Mexicans had won the battle.

DID YOU KNOW?

Porfirio Díaz led the cavalry at the Battle of Puebla. In 1863, he was captured by the French army. He escaped.

Porfirio Díaz became the president of Mexico in 1876.

Words of Hope

★ ★

After the battle, fighting went on for five more years.

The Battle of Puebla was a great victory for the Mexican people, but it did not end the war. Fighting went on for five more years. During that time, the Mexican people thought about Puebla. They believed that if they had beaten the French once, they could do it again. *El Cinco de Mayo*, or "the fifth of May," became a symbol of Mexican strength and unity.

In 1867, their hopes came true. The French were forced to leave Mexico. Today, Cinco de Mayo is a national holiday in Mexico and the United States.

★ ★ ★ ★ ★ ★ ★ ★

Some Mexicans march in parades during Cinco de Mayo celebrations in Mexico City.

Zaragoza's Speech

Before the Battle of Puebla, General Zaragoza gave a speech. His words cheered the Mexican soldiers. "Your enemies are the first soldiers of the world, but you are the first sons of Mexico. They wish to seize your Fatherland, Soldiers! I read victory and faith on your foreheads. Long live ndependence! Long live the Fatherland!" Later, these same words gave hope to the Mexican people.

Our Lady of Loreto Chapel is at the Presidio La Bahia near Goliad, Texas. General Zaragoza was born in the town that surrounded the presidio, or fort.

Creating the Holiday

Many people in the United States celebrate Cinco de Mayo.

In the 1860s, the United States helped Mexico win the war against the French. They gave the Mexicans weapons. Some Americans even joined the Mexican army. Many states, such as Texas and California, had once belonged to Mexico. Many Mexicans lived in these areas but still felt very close to Mexico. When Mexico won the war, people in the United States were happy. They began celebrating Cinco de Mayo, too. Today, some of these communities have been celebrating this holiday for more than 100 years.

DID YOU KNOW?

Mexico and the United States were at war from 1846 to 1848. The United States took some of Mexico's land. When the war ended, the two countries decided not to fight again.

Children make masks to wear for Cinco de Mayo celebrations.

Today, Cinco de Mayo is a bigger holiday in the United States than it is in Mexico. More people celebrate it every year. It is not just for Mexican Americans. Other **Hispanic** groups, such as Cubans and Puerto Ricans, see May 5 as a day to celebrate their cultures. Many non-Hispanic people also enjoy this holiday. It is a chance for them to have fun and learn about Mexican culture.

Some Mexicans take part in plays about the Battle of Puebla. They wear clothing or hats in the same colors as the flag of Mexico.

Celebrating Today

Many Cinco de Mayo celebrations include carnivals and fairs.

Cinco de Mayo is most often celebrated with a *fiesta*. Eating special foods, such as *gorditas*, *menudo*, and *buñuelos*, is an important part of Cinco de Mayo. Celebrating with music and dance is also part of many events. *Mariachi* bands stroll through the crowds singing Mexican folk songs. *Ballet folklórico* dancers wear colorful costumes. *Jalisco* dancers perform dances with large, circular motions. People also perform the *jarabe tapatio*, or the Mexican Hat Dance. It is the national dance of Mexico.

Many Cinco de Mayo celebrations include carnivals and fairs. People play games and buy crafts. Parades with brightly colored floats wind through the streets. One of the most exciting parts of Cinco de Mayo happens after dark. That is when a colorful display of fireworks lights up the night sky.

DID YOU KNOW?

A fiesta is a party. It can last one day, three days, or even a whole week. The word *fiesta* means "feast day" in Spanish.

14

Men and women wear traditional clothing and perform dances during Cinco de Mayo fiestas.

Americans Celebrate

More than 500 cities across the United States have official Cinco de Mayo celebrations. This map shows a few of the events that take place across the country on May 5.

Los Angeles, California, has the largest Cinco de Mayo celebration in the country. It takes up 36 city blocks, and more than 500,000 people attend. Each year, the mayor of the city gives a speech in Spanish.

Denver, Colorado

Los Angeles, California

Kona has celebrated Cinco de Mayo for more than 20 years. Mexican people have been living in Hawai'i since the 1830s. At that time, Mexican cowboys moved there from California.

0   100   200   300 miles

Kona, Hawai'i

General Ignacio Zaragoza was born in Goliad, Texas. A 3,000-pound statue of him sits in the town square. It was a gift from Puebla to Texas. In 1999, Goliad was named the official site of Cinco de Mayo for the whole state.

In Minnesota, more than 100,000 visitors regularly attend St. Paul's Cinco de Mayo celebration. It takes place every year in the city's District del Sol neighborhood. Visitors enjoy a parade, dancing, music, food, and even a car show.

St. Paul's, Minnesota

More than half of all Mexicans in New York are *poblanos*. This means that they or their parents were born in the state of Puebla, Mexico. New York celebrates Cinco de Mayo every year with a fiesta in Flushing Meadow Park. Many people attend, including the governor of the state.

New York

Denver's Cinco de Mayo festival began in 1987. Today, about 500,000 people attend each year. At Civic Center Park, visitors enjoy arts and crafts, storytelling, a car show, and sports displays, including inline skating, skateboarding, and BMX biking.

Goliad, Texas

Holiday Symbols

Cinco de Mayo is one of the *Fiestas Patrias*, or **"Patriotic Festivals"** in Mexican culture. These holidays are a chance for people to feel proud. They show their pride with special patriotic symbols.

★ ★ ★ ★ ★ ★ ★ ★ ★

The Mexican flag has a picture of an eagle with a snake in its beak. Aztec legend says that the gods told their people to build a city where they saw an eagle and a serpent. This is now Mexico City.

The Mexican Flag

Mexico's flag is made up of three bands of color. Green is on the left, white is in the middle, and red is on the right. Each color has a special meaning. The green band represents independence. The white band symbolizes religion. The red band stands for unity. At Cinco de Mayo festivals, these colors can be seen everywhere.

Fireworks

Most Mexican fiestas begin with the sound of *fuegos artificiales*, or fireworks, shattering the sky. Fireworks signal that something special is about to begin. On Cinco de Mayo, fireworks light up the sky a second time after dark. Just like on the Fourth of July, they signal a happy end to a day of celebrating.

Piñatas

Piñatas are papier-mâché containers filled with treats. The Spanish brought piñatas to Mexico nearly 400 years ago. During a fiesta, a piñata is hung from a tree. Children are blindfolded, and they take turns trying to break the piñata with a stick. The parents move the piñata up and down with a rope. When the piñata breaks, treats spill out, and the children pick up the prizes.

Further Research

These books and websites can help you learn more about Cinco de Mayo in Mexico and the United States.

Websites

Find out more about celebrating Cinco de Mayo at:

www.howstuffworks.com

Type "Cinco de Mayo" in the search box, and click "Go".

Try searching for Cinco de Mayo and the Battle of Puebla at:

www.elbalero.gob.mx

Books

Gnojewski, Carol. *Cinco de Mayo Crafts*. Berkley Heights: Enslow Publishing, 2005.

Heinrichs, Ann and Kathleen Petelinsek. *Cinco de Mayo*. Chanhassen: Child's World, 2006.

Crafts and Recipes

Make your own Piñata

Have an adult blow up a balloon and knot the end. In a large mixing bowl, stir two cups of flour into three cups of water to form a paste. Tear old newspapers into one-inch strips. Dip the strips into the paste, and wrap them around the balloon. Leave some of the balloon uncovered at the knotted end. Allow the coating to dry completely.

Once it is dry, decorate your piñata with streamers and colored paper.

Snip a hole in the knotted end of the balloon. Remove the broken balloon. Fill the piñata with small surprises, such as candy or stickers. Stuff the hole with crunched up newspaper, and seal with tape. Make a loop for hanging the piñata by attaching twine to either end of the opening. Ask an adult to help you find a safe place to hang your piñata. Then play the piñata game with your friends.

Cinco de Mayo Recipe

Mexican Hot Chocolate

Have an adult help you make this treat.

Ingredients:

2 ounces unsweetened
chocolate
2 cups milk
1 cup heavy cream
6 tablespoons sugar
1/2 teaspoon cinnamon

Equipment:

saucepan
wooden spoon
cup

1. Melt the chocolate in a saucepan.
2. In a separate pot, warm milk and cream on a low heat until hot. Do not burn the liquid.
3. Add a bit of hot milk to the melted chocolate, and mix to form a paste.
4. Then stir in the remaining milk mixture, sugar, and cinnamon.
5. Serve and enjoy.

Holiday Quiz

What have you learned about Cinco de Mayo? See if you can answer the following questions. Check your answers on the next page.

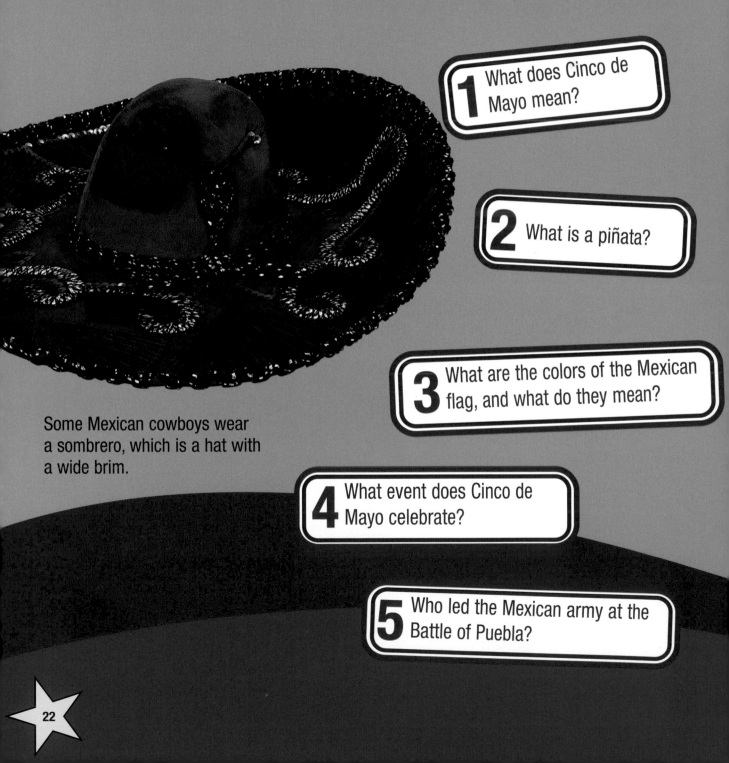

1 What does Cinco de Mayo mean?

2 What is a piñata?

3 What are the colors of the Mexican flag, and what do they mean?

Some Mexican cowboys wear a sombrero, which is a hat with a wide brim.

4 What event does Cinco de Mayo celebrate?

5 Who led the Mexican army at the Battle of Puebla?

Fascinating Facts

★ The French invasion of Mexico was the last time any place on mainland North or South America was invaded by a country outside of North or South America.

★ Today, Cinco de Mayo is the biggest Hispanic holiday in the United States.

★ During Cinco de Mayo celebrations, Americans eat more than 50 million avocados. Most of these are used to make guacamole, a traditional Mexican dip.

★ Today, the site of the Battle of Puebla is a city park. There is also a museum with a display of toy soldiers showing what happened on May 5, 1862.

Quiz Answers:
1. *Cinco de Mayo* means "fifth of May" in Spanish. This is also the day that the holiday takes place.
2. A piñata is a papier-mâché container filled with treats.
3. The colors on the Mexican flag are green, white, and red. Green stands for independence, white for religion, and red for unity.
4. Cinco de Mayo celebrates the victory of the Mexican army over the French at the Battle of Puebla.
5. General Ignacio Zaragoza led the army.

Glossary

ballet folklórico: Mexican folk dance

buñuelos: deep-fried pastries that are similar to doughnuts

cavalry: troops who fight on horseback

gorditas: thick tortillas stuffed with meat, vegetables, or cheese

Hispanic: of, or related to, Spanish-speaking peoples

Jalisco: a state in Mexico

mariachi: a type of music played by a Mexican band

Mestizo: people who have mixed Spanish and American Indian backgrounds

patriotic: having a feeling of pride for one's country

Zapotec: American Indian group from Central America

Index